The Biography of Tea

Carrie Gleason

Crabtree Publishing Company
www.crabtreebooks.com

Crabtree Publishing Company

www.crabtreebooks.com

For my surly, Scottish Poodle. Love, Rosie xoxo

Coordinating editor: Ellen Rodger
Editors: Rachel Eagen, Adrianna Morganelli, L. Michelle Nielsen
Production manager: Rosie Gowsell
Production assistance: Samara Parent
Art direction: Rob MacGregor
Photo research: Allison Napier
Prepress technician: Nancy Johnson

Photo Credits: Steve Cavalier/Alamy: p. 6 (bottom); Bryan & Cherry Alexander Photography/Alamy: p. 21 (bottom); Paul Cowan/Alamy: p. 27 (middle); DAJ/Alamy: p. 7 (bottom); Kevin Lang/Alamy: p. 1; Kirsty McLaren/Alamy: p. 26 (top), p. 27 (bottom), p. 31 (bottom); Miamnuk Images/Alamy: p. 27 (top); David Pearson/Alamy: p. 6 (top), p. 26 (bottom); Amoret Tanner/Alamy: 13 (top); Sam Toren/Alamy: p. 31 (top); Clive Tully/Alamy: p. 20 (left); Gari Wyn Williams/Alamy: p. 14 (bottom); Worldwide Picture Library/Alamy: p. 9; Werner Forman/Art Resource, NY: p. 12 (bottom); HIP/Art Resource, NY: p. 12 (top); Erich Lessing/Art Resource, NY: p. 29 (bottom); SEF/Art Resource, NY: p. 11 (top); Bibliotheque Nationale, Paris, France, Lauros/Giraudon/The Bridgeman Art Library: p. 10; Chinese School/Societe Asiatique, College de France, Paris, France, Archives Charmet/The Bridgeman Art Library: p. 10; Private Collection, The Stapleton Collection/The Bridgeman Art Library: p. 4; State Art Museum, Nizhny Novgorod, Russia/The Bridgeman Art Library: p. 13; Dean Conger/Corbis: p. 7 (top); Corbis: p. 17 (top); P.Desgrieux/photocuisine/Corbis: p. 5 (top); Lindsay Hebberd/Corbis: p. 25; Karen Kasmauski/Corbis: p. 24; Phil Schermeister/Corbis: p. 23; Swim Ink 2, LLC/Corbis: p. 19 (top); The Granger Collection, New York: p. 5 (bottom), p. 16 (bottom), p. 17 (bottom), p. 22 (left); Chapman/The Image Works: p. 30 (top); Gardenworldimages/Jenny Lilly/The Image Works: p. 22 (right); Mary Evans Picture Library/The Image Works: p. 14 (top), p. 15 (bottom); Mary Evans/The Women's Library/The Image Works: p. 18; NMPFT/Kodak Collection/SSPL/The Image Works: p. 20 (top); Topham/The Image Works: p. 19 (bottom), p. 21 (middle), p. 28 (bottom); North Wind/North Wind Picture Archives: p. 15; Mark Henley/Panos Pictures: p. 28 (top); Chris Stowers/Panos Pictures: cover; Dr. Jeremy Burgess/Photo Researchers, Inc.: p. 16 (top); Food and Drug Administration/Photo Researchers, Inc.: p. 30 (bottom). Other images from stock photo Cd.

Cartography: Jim Chernishenko: p. 8

Cover: A woman harvests tea leaves in the highlands of Sri Lanka. Sri Lanka is a tropical island country located off the southern coast of India. Sri Lanka used to be called Ceylon. Tea from Sri Lanka is still sometimes called Ceylon tea.

Title page: A hot drink vender in Syria sells tea, which he makes using a type of teapot called a samovar.

Contents: Very small pieces of tea leaves, called fannings, are used in tea bags.

Library and Archives Canada Cataloguing in Publication

Gleason, Carrie, 1973-
  The biography of tea / Carrie Gleason.

(How did that get here?)
Includes index.
ISBN 978-0-7787-2493-3 (bound)
ISBN 978-0-7787-2529-9 (pbk.)

  1. Tea--Juvenile literature. I. Title. II. Series.

SB271.G44 2007   j633.7'2   C2007-900697-3

Library of Congress Cataloging-in-Publication Data

Gleason, Carrie, 1973-
  The Biography of tea / written by Carrie Gleason.
    p. cm. -- (How did that get here?)
  Includes index.
  ISBN-13: 978-0-7787-2493-3 (rlb)
  ISBN-10: 0-7787-2493-X (rlb)
  ISBN-13: 978-0-7787-2529-9 (pb.)
  ISBN-10: 0-7787-2529-4 (pb.)
  1. Tea--Juvenile literature. 2. Tea trade--Juvenile literature. I. Title. II. Series.

SB271.G54 2007
633.7'2--dc22
                     2007003459

Crabtree Publishing Company

www.crabtreebooks.com   1-800-387-7650

Published in Canada
Crabtree Publishing
616 Welland Ave.
St. Catharines, ON
L2M 5V6

Published in the United States
Crabtree Publishing
PMB16A
350 Fifth Ave., Suite 3308
New York, NY 10118

Published in the United Kingdom
Crabtree Publishing
White Cross Mills
High Town, Lancaster
LA1 4XS

Published in Australia
Crabtree Publishing
386 Mt. Alexander Rd.
Ascot Vale (Melbourne)
VIC 3032

Contents

Tea Time

Tea is the second most popular drink in the world, after water. People started drinking tea thousands of years ago in ancient China. Since then, it has become an important part of daily life in many cultures. In Japan, tea began as a beverage that **monks** drank to help them concentrate during **meditation**. Hundreds of years later, the act of serving and drinking tea in Japan has developed into a well-known ceremony that is a part of Japanese culture. In England, tea grew from a beverage enjoyed only by the wealthy to become a **staple** of the British **working class**. Tea came to be associated with the British so much that American **colonists** boycotted, or refused to buy, the drink during the late 1700s to show their displeasure over British rule.

Flavor Infusion

Tea is an infusion drink made from the leaves of an **evergreen shrub** commonly called the tea plant. The leaves are infused, or soaked in hot water until their flavor is released. The flowers, stems, and leaves of plants other than the tea plant, such as peppermint and chamomile plants, are also made into hot drinks. These drinks are called tisanes. Tisanes are sometimes mistakenly called tea, but they are not tea because they do not contain leaves from the tea plant.

▼ *Tea plants have dark green leaves and small white flowers.*

4

The Tea Trade

The worldwide popularity of tea has made it an important commodity today. A commodity is a product or good that is bought and sold on world **markets**. Throughout its history, tea has reached **consumers** by being shipped overland on camel caravans, across oceans on fast sailing ships called tea clippers, and most recently, in modern cargo ships. Tea has been used in many ways. It has been shaped into bricks and used as currency, and ground into dust that is packaged into tea bags and sold at corner stores. Tea is **processed** to suit different tastes, and often has milk, sugar, spices, and even ice added to it. Today, approximately 30 billion cups of tea are drunk around the world every day.

▶ *Different types of tea are made from the tea plant. The main types are green tea, black tea, and oolong tea. These teas differ in the way they are processed.*

(below) Tea has become a part of the culture of many countries. In this illustration from the British children's book Alice in Wonderland, the "Hatter" throws a tea party.

The Tea Plant

Tea comes from the leaves and **buds** of evergreen shrubs called tea plants. Two main types of tea plants are cultivated, or grown as crops, in the world today. They are the China tea plant, or *Camellia sinensis* and the Assam or India tea plant, called *Camellia assamica*. Tea plants first grew in the Himalaya mountains, between what is now India and Tibet, in Asia.

Types of Tea Plants

China tea plants can grow up to 30 feet (nine meters) tall when they are left to grow wild. On tea farms, the trees are pruned, or cut back, into shrubs about six feet (two meters) tall. Today, these plants are cultivated, or grown as a crop, in China, Tibet, and Japan. *Camellia assamica* is a tea tree that comes from Assam, a state in northeast India. This type of tea plant grows up to 60 feet (18 meters) tall in the wild and has larger leaves than the Chinese tea plant. It is grown on farms mainly in India and other Southeast Asian countries. The trees are pruned into shrubs to encourage new shoots, or stems to grow. Young leaves from these shoots are harvested to make tea.

(above) Tea plants are pruned into shrubs and grown on plantations such as this one in southern India.

▶ *The top leaves of tea plants are harvested to make the best teas.*

Tea Leaves and the Body

Tea leaves contain different chemicals. Some of these, such as a chemical called tannin, give tea its slightly bitter taste. Scientists believe that the plants produce the chemicals to deter animals and insects from feeding on them. Caffeine is another chemical found in tea leaves. Caffeine is a stimulant, which means that when people consume caffeine, they feel more alert. Too much caffeine can make people feel nervous or cause headaches. Unlike other caffeinated beverages, such as coffee and soda pop, the caffeine in tea is released slowly and stays in the body longer. This helps people feel the effects of tea's caffeine more gently. Flavonoids are other naturally occurring chemicals found in tea leaves. These chemicals work as antioxidants in the body, which means that they help keep **cells** from being damaged. Damaged cells lead to diseases. Some of these chemicals, as well as vitamins and minerals found in tea leaves, make tea a healthy drink.

(above) All types of tea contain caffeine, but in different amounts. Black tea has the most caffeine, followed by oolong, and then green tea. Tea can also be decaffeinated, or have most of its caffeine removed, during processing.

Tea's Magical Powers

Many legends surround the discovery and early uses of tea. One legend from India explains why tea stimulates the body, or gives drinkers an energy boost. In the legend, a **Buddhist** monk named Daruma fell asleep one day while meditating. When Daruma awoke, he was furious with himself for falling asleep. He tore off his eyelids and threw them to the ground. A tea plant grew where Daruma's eyelids landed. The tea plant became the source of the drink that would keep future generations of Buddhist monks awake during meditation.

◄ *A doll of Daruma.*

Tea Lands

Tea plants grow in the tropics and subtropics, which are areas of the world with warm **climates**. Tea plants cannot survive in extreme temperatures. Both high heat and frost can kill the plants. Most tea plants are grown in tropical highlands. Tropical highlands are areas of the tropics with high **elevation** and cool weather. Tea plants can withstand temperatures as low as 20°F (6°C), which keeps the leaves small to produce better tasting tea. In tropical highlands, the plants also receive plenty of rain. Tea plants need at least 45 inches (one meter) of rain per year. Some varieties of tea plants can grow in areas of low elevation.

Types of Tea Gardens

Tea is grown as a cash crop, which means that it is grown to be sold, and not to be consumed locally. Most tea is grown on plantations. Plantations are large farms that usually grow one crop on a large scale and employ many people. In India, most tea is grown on plantations. Other tea bushes are grown on smallholder farms, which are smaller, family-owned farms. Many smallholder farms are found in China. Tea farms are sometimes called tea gardens or tea estates, regardless of their size.

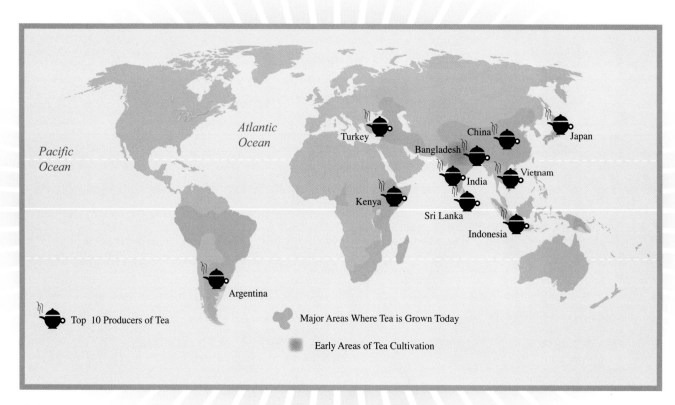

(above) Tea is grown in over 40 countries. This map shows the top tea producing countries. India consumes the most tea.

Top of Tea Mountain

China is the world's top producer of tea. Tea is one of China's most important **exports**. India is the world's second-largest producer, employing nearly two million people to work in its tea industry. India has three main tea-growing regions. Assam is one major tea-producing region. It is located at the foothills of the Himalaya mountains, and its soil is fed by nutrients from annual flooding of the Brahmaputra River. Other areas of India that produce a lot of tea are Darjeeling in the north and the Nilgiri Hills, or "Blue Mountains," in the southwest.

Other Top Producers

Sri Lanka is the third-largest producer of tea. Sri Lankan tea plantations are located in the mountains at the center of the island. Tea has been an important export in Kenya, the fourth-largest producer, since the 1950s. Tea grows in the central highlands of Kenya, while most of the rest of the country is too dry for growing tea. Tea is also grown in other countries with tropical climates, such as Indonesia, Japan, and Vietnam.

(above) Tea grown on mountainsides is planted on terraces, or flat "steps" of land carved into hillsides.

All the Tea in China

Most historians believe traders spread tea through China. At first, tea was drunk in **temples** and **monasteries**. Monks accepted the drink because the caffeine kept them alert for meditation and prayer. Until around 300 A.D., tea was mainly used as medicine by everyone else. Around 400 A.D., tea began to be cultivated, or grown, on farms in southern China. Chinese farmers paid tea as tribute, or tax, to the emperor, or ruler. Over time, tea came to be served in taverns and shops that also served noodles. Merchants **prospered** from the sale of tea, and potters, silversmiths, and goldsmiths began to make and sell dishes for drinking and storing tea.

(above) During the Tang Dynasty (618 to 907 A.D.), tea grew in popularity. In this painting, the Emperor receives tribute, including tea, from the people.

The Emperor's Tea

According to an ancient Chinese legend, Emperor Shen Nung, who was known as "the father of agriculture," ruled China more than 4,000 years ago. One day in 2737 B.C., he was resting under a tea tree while his servant boiled water for him to drink. As the servant passed him the drink, tea leaves from above fell into the water. Shen Nung liked the drink so much that he ordered tea to be cultivated all over China.

Emperor Shen Nung studied many plants. He is also believed to be the "founder of medicine."

Bricks, Powder, and Leaves

In ancient China, tea was prepared from tea bricks, or cakes. To make tea bricks, the leaves were steamed and crushed, then mixed into a paste that was held together by plum juice, and, sometimes, by animal dung. The mixture was poured into molds and baked. When it was time to prepare the tea for drinking, the tea brick was roasted in a fire to soften it, then boiling water was poured over it. Another way of preparing tea was to crush the tea cake into a powder, then whisk the powder with hot water to create a frothy beverage. During China's Ming Dynasty (1368 to 1644), the way tea was prepared changed from being a frothy drink made from powdered tea to an infused drink make from tea leaves. Tea leaves were left loose rather than formed into bricks. Chinese farmers also began to process tea in different forms, including black tea, which was exported. To make black tea, the leaves were **fermented**, and then baked to preserve them, or prevent them from rotting. This kept the tea fresh for longer journeys.

Tea Trade

Tea bricks were shaped into a **standard** size and carried by merchants to trade, as well as to eat and drink on long voyages. Tea and other Chinese goods, such as silk and **porcelain**, were traded on the Silk Road. The Silk Road was a series of trade routes that spread west from China, across Central Asia to the Middle East. Another trade route, called Chamadao, or "the tea and horse road" started in southwest China, where many tea farms were located, and led north through the mountains of Tibet and into India. On this route, tea, sugar, and salt were traded for Tibetan horses, cows, and furs.

(above) Tea houses and tea rooms were opened in China where tea masters were judged by the way they brewed and served tea in ceremonies.

▶ *To add extra flavor to tea, spices such as cloves and cardamom, and plants and herbs, such as onions, orange peel, and peppermint, were added.*

Tea Spreads

During the late 1400s, Europeans began setting out on voyages of discovery. They were looking for new lands to claim and riches to trade. Some of the most sought-after items were spices from what is now Indonesia, and silk and porcelain from China.

▶ *An ancient Chinese pot for carrying tea. Chinese tea was traded as far as Kenya, Africa.*

(top) A tea warehouse in China. The tea trade grew after Europeans were introduced to the beverage.

China's Visitors

In 1517, the Portuguese became the first Europeans to reach China by sea. Portuguese traders paid tribute to the Chinese emperor to be allowed to trade in China. By the mid-1500s, Portuguese traders had set up a permanent trading post in Macao, in southern China. Through Macao, the Portuguese controlled all trade of Chinese goods to Europe, and the Chinese could tax and monitor all goods leaving the country. By 1559, reports of tea, a strange new beverage, reached Europe. Historians believe that Portuguese sailors may have brought small amounts of tea to Lisbon, Portugal's capital city.

The Tea Trade in Europe

The Dutch were the first to bring a large shipment of tea to Europe. In 1602, the Dutch East India Company was established to handle the trade between Asia and the Netherlands. The Dutch East India Company was a group of merchants and **investors** who received permission from the government for a **monopoly** over trade in Asia. In 1610, a Dutch East India ship brought a shipment of tea to the Netherlands. There, tea quickly grew popular among all **social classes**. Dutch companies sold the tea to Italy, France, and Germany. In France, tea was introduced around 1630, but only the wealthy wanted to drink it. Most French people thought of tea as a "women's drink." Tea was first introduced to England in the 1650s.

Russian Camel Caravans

Tea first reached Russia as a gift from the Chinese to the Russian Tzar, or king, Alexis, in 1618. As tea became more popular in Russia, regular trade developed between the two countries. Trade caravans of up to 300 camels laden with Russian furs left western Russia and traveled up to eight months to reach the Russian-Chinese border where trading posts had been set up. Eight months later, the camels returned, each carrying up to 600 pounds (272 kg) of tea. Until the 1800s, tea that reached Europe via camel caravans was believed to be better than tea that had traveled on ships. It was thought that the humidity, or moisture in the air, from ocean travel ruined the flavor of the tea. By the early 1800s, Russia was the largest consumer of tea after China.

▲ *An advertisement for a tea named after the Russian camel caravans. Russian camel caravans lasted until roads and canals were built in the 1900s.*

(left) When tea arrived in western Russia, it was sold at the Nizhni Novgorod fair, or market.

▲ *In 1662, England's King Charles II married a Portuguese princess named Catherine of Braganza. She is credited with making tea popular in England's royal court. Women in England followed her example and started to drink tea as well.*

Tea and Coffee

In England, tea was first served in coffeehouses. Coffeehouses were early coffee shops where men gathered to drink, talk, and do business. Tea was made and stored in barrels until a customer asked for it. The cold tea was then drawn from the barrel and reheated. Tea was a luxury drink that sold for as much as ten dollars a pound, so only the wealthy could afford to buy it. In the early 1700s, a direct trade in tea between England and China began when England's merchant company, the British East India Company, decided to import tea in large amounts. The British government imposed a high tax on tea. Even though the tax made it expensive, tea began to be popular among people of all social classes. Members of England's poorer classes sometimes bought used tea from the wealthy. Smugglers brought tea to England illegally, which caused the British East India Company to lose money because they could not sell their more expensive tea legally. By the time the British government lowered the tax on tea in 1784, the British East India Company had an oversupply of tea that it needed to get rid of.

Debating Health Effects

One of the first London coffeehouses to sell tea was owned by Thomas Garway, in 1657. To get more people interested in buying tea, Garway published a pamphlet that claimed that tea purified the blood, liver, bladder, and kidneys, and drove away fears and improved memory. Some doctors debated that tea was bad for people's health, leading to **convulsions** and **epilepsy**. Other doctors and scientists supported Chinese beliefs that tea was a healthy drink. In 1679, one Dutch physician wrote that people who were sick should drink 100 cups of tea a day until they were better!

▲ *In 1717, Thomas Twining converted his London coffeehouse into a tea room, which admitted both men and women. Today, Twinings is an English tea company that sells its tea throughout Europe and North America.*

The Boston Tea Party

The British East India Company was given permission by the British government to export its extra tea to Britain's North American colonies. At that time, Britain ruled 13 colonies in what is now the eastern United States. The colonists were already angry with the British government over taxation. Granting the British East India Company control over the import of tea to the colonies threatened the business of colonial tea merchants. The colonists boycotted, or refused to drink tea. In 1773, seven ships carrying tea from England entered the American ports of New York, Philadelphia, Boston, and Charleston. In Boston, Massachusetts, American colonists boarded one of the ships and dumped the tea overboard. In retaliation, the British government closed the Boston harbor, enraging the colonists. This event helped unite the 13 colonies to fight for their independence from Britain.

(above) In Boston, colonists dressed as Native Americans dumped tea into the harbor.

Tea Clippers

Until the early 1800s, tea took at least a year to reach London from China on British East India Company ships. The British East India Company used ships called "East Indiamen" that were slow and heavy. To improve speed, shipbuilders made fast sailing ships called "clippers." These ships were smaller, lighter, and had more sails than other sailing ships of the time, and could make the round trip from New York to China and back again in less than eight months. Clipper ships that were used in the tea trade came to be called "tea clippers, or "China Clippers." Clipper ships raced to see which ship was fastest. The ship that won the race could sell its tea first, and make the most money.

◂ *Tea clipper races became a sport that people bet money on.*

Tea Plantations

During the 1700s, all of England's tea came from China. Around 1840, China refused to sell the British any more tea, so the British looked to their Asian colonies. The British, as well as the Dutch, Portuguese, and other European countries, had set up colonies in the lands they had explored. Europeans went to the colonies to extract whatever resources they could from the land, and grow crops on plantations. Colonists who owned plantations were called planters.

◄ *The Chinese refused to trade with the British during the Opium Wars. The Chinese government tried to ban the drug, made from poppies, but the British East India Company continued to sell it illegally in China, which led to wars.*

Indian Tea

In 1823, two employees of the British East India Company discovered that people in India drank tea made from the Assam tea plant. They established a tea plantation in northeast India and shipped the tea back to England. Tea plantations in India were soon started by British planters in Darjeeling and other areas of northern India. British planters needed workers to grow and harvest their tea, so they brought in hundreds of people from southern India. The workers lived on plantations in poor housing supplied by plantation owners. The workers received very little pay and worked nine hours a day, six days a week. Managers, who oversaw the day-to-day operations, were English. After India gained independence from Britain in 1847, new labor laws were established which required tea plantations to provide schools and medical care for workers and their families.

Indentured laborers working as tea harvesters in Ceylon in 1883. Tea harvesters had their baskets of picked tea leaves weighed at the end of each day. They were paid according to weight of the basket.

British Planters in Ceylon

British planters in Ceylon, now Sri Lanka, also established tea plantations. British planters grew coffee there until a disease wiped out the crop in 1869. A planter named James Taylor was the first to plant tea instead. Thirty years later, Ceylon was a major producer of tea. By 1901, the British were consuming about 260 million pounds of tea per year. Most of this tea came from its colonies in India and Ceylon. The tea plantations were worked by indentured laborers from India. British planters looked to India for a cheap supply of labor. Indentured laborers had their passage from India to Sri Lanka paid for by the planters, but once they arrived, they were forced to work for a specific period of time under a contract. They were not allowed to leave the plantation and worked to repay the money it had cost to bring them there.

▶ *British grocer Thomas Lipton bought plantations in Ceylon so that he would have a steady supply of tea to sell in his stores, without having to pay to import it. Today, Lipton is a popular tea company.*

Tea in Africa

Tea plantations were established in British colonies in Kenya in the early 1900s. In Cameroon and Tanzania, German planters set up plantations between 1884 and 1914. In Malawi, tea plant seeds from Ceylon were planted in 1900. In South Africa, seeds from Ceylon were also planted in 1877. Many African tea plantations were broken into smallholder farms after the countries achieved independence.

Tea Culture Around the World

Today, the largest consumer of tea per capita, or per person, is the United Kingdom, which includes England, Scotland, Wales, and Northern Ireland. In these, as well as other countries around the world, tea has become an important part of the culture.

Afternoon Tea

In the United Kingdom, afternoon tea is a social event believed to have started in the early 1800s by an English Duchess. The Duchess found that during the long time gap between lunch and the late evening meal, she grew hungry and weak. She asked her servants to bring her tea and a light snack in her room. Soon, she asked her friends to join her. This developed into the British custom of afternoon tea, or "low tea" in which a small snack and tea is consumed in the late afternoon.

(above) Women having afternoon tea at an outdoor garden party in England in the 1920s. Many etiquette, or proper behavior, books were written about the appropriate way to serve and drink tea.

Earl Grey Tea

Earl Grey tea is a type of tea named after a British Prime Minister. It is a blend, or mix of teas flavored with the oil of a citrus fruit called bergamot. There are different versions of the story of how the tea blend got its name. According to one version, a British diplomat in China received the ingredients for the tea blend after saving the life of a Chinese man. The diplomat passed on the recipe to British Prime Minister Earl Grey, and the drink was named after him. Today, it is one of the most popular forms of black tea.

High Tea

By the Industrial Revolution, a period of English history beginning in the mid-1700s, when more people worked at machines in factories, tea became a drink of the working class, who took "tea breaks." For the people who worked in factories and mines, the main evening meal came to be called "tea," or "high tea." It was called tea because the workers finished their workday around the same time that the wealthy were having their afternoon tea.

Tea Gardens, Shops, and Dances

After England's coffeehouses closed in the early 1700s, tea gardens were opened. In tea gardens, men, women, and children of all social classes enjoyed the day, strolling through flower gardens, listening to outdoor concerts, and drinking tea. Teashops were places where people shopped, but which also had a few tables where people could sit and have tea and a snack. The first teashop was opened in England in 1864. The manager of a bakery in London opened a room at the back of the store for people to have tea. Soon, companies that sold other products, such as tobacco, tea, and cakes, also opened teashops in their stores. These shops served hot and cold foods, tea, and often provided musical entertainment. Tea dances became popular in the early 1900s in England, when people began socializing more outside their homes. Hotels began serving more elaborate afternoon teas, with three courses, or meals. At the same time, the tango, a dance from Argentina, was becoming popular in London. The dances were organized to coincide with tea time.

A tea company advertisement from the late 1800s.

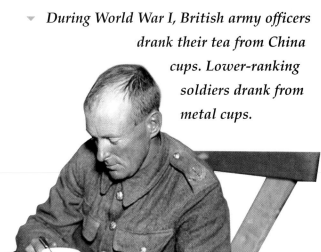

During World War I, British army officers drank their tea from China cups. Lower-ranking soldiers drank from metal cups.

(above) Tea was a symbol of the temperance movement. The temperance movement was an attempt to stop people from drinking alcoholic beverages in the 1800s. Temperance leaders held tea parties and rallies to raise money for their cause.

China from China

When tea was first imported to Europe, it was sold with small teapots from China. The porcelain pots and cups where shipped with the tea to add weight to ships to make them more stable at sea because the chests of tea were very light. The pottery pieces were then sold to people in Europe, and came to be called "china." In China, tea was boiled with water in open pots and then poured into smaller cups, which did not have handles, for drinking. When tea began to be prepared as an infusion drink, which means that hot water was poured over the tea which was then left to steep, or soak, a spout and lid were added to teapots. Over time, tea sets in Europe became more elaborate and decorative. The British added spoons, sugar bowls, milk jugs, and saucers to hold the spoons, to form tea sets.

Tea Bags

European colonists first introduced tea to North America. It was a popular beverage in large cities, such as New York, Boston, and Philadelphia, where it was drunk in tea gardens and coffeehouses. In 1908, a New York tea merchant named Thomas Sullivan invented tea bags. He sent out small samples of tea in loosely woven silk bags that could be used to brew tea. Later, gauze and then paper replaced silk as tea bag material. In North America, tea bags are the main way of brewing tea today.

▲ *In Russia, tea is traditionally prepared in a vessel called a samovar. A samovar is a large metal kettle, usually made from copper or brass.*

Tea Chills Out

Iced tea is strong, brewed tea that is served over ice. Iced tea was first served in 1904 at the St. Louis **World's Fair**. At that time, most tea consumed in the United States was green tea from China. Tea producers from India set up a pavilion to try and get Americans interested in drinking black tea from India. The temperature outside during the fair was very hot, and people did not want to try the tea. The man in charge of the pavilion, Richard Blechynden, packed ice cubes into glasses and poured tea into them to make iced tea. Customers tried the cool, refreshing drink and iced tea became a success. One hundred years later, Americans were drinking almost 2 billion glasses of iced tea a year. Most of the tea consumed in the United States today is iced tea. Tea is also made into flavored drinks by soda pop companies in the United States.

One Lump or Two?

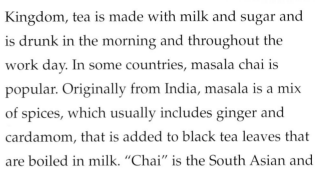

Tea is prepared in many different ways around the world. In the United Kingdom, tea is made with milk and sugar and is drunk in the morning and throughout the work day. In some countries, masala chai is popular. Originally from India, masala is a mix of spices, which usually includes ginger and cardamom, that is added to black tea leaves that are boiled in milk. "Chai" is the South Asian and Middle Eastern word for tea. In Russia, tea is drunk with jam or sugar. A spoonful of either is eaten and a drink of tea follows.

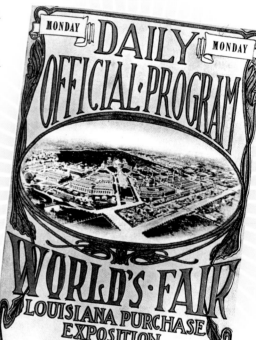

(below) A nomadic family in Siberia, in northern Russia, take a tea break. They drink tea with reindeer milk and salt.

▲ *Iced tea was first introduced in St. Louis at the 1904 World's Fair.*

The Japanese Tea Ceremony

Tea was introduced to Japan around 600 A.D. At first it was drunk by Buddhist monks in monasteries. Around 800 A.D., a monk named Dengyo Daishi brought tea plant seeds from China to Japan and planted them in the garden of his monastery. When the leaves were ready, he sent them to the Japanese Emperor, Saga. Saga is said to have liked the tea so much that he ordered tea to be cultivated in Japan. Tea consumption in Japan began to rise.

Beginnings

In 1191, a Buddhist monk named Eisai returned to Japan after visiting China. Eisai wrote a book called Kissa-yojo-ki, or "Notes on the Curative Effects of Tea." In the book, he told of tea's medicinal powers. The book reached Sanetomo, the Shogun, or military leader of Japan. Sanetomo was suffering from a stomach illness. Eisai's method of making tea cured him. Eisai's method of tea preparation included instructions on how to pick, prepare, and drink a powdered green tea called matcha. Teahouses and tea stalls sprung up all over Japan and people also began to grow tea plants in their home gardens.

(above) A modern-day Japanese tea room.

◄ A historial image of a girl serving tea in a Japanese tea room.

Zen and Tea

By 1400, the steps of tea preparation laid out by Eisai had evolved into a tea ceremony. The tea ceremony was greatly influenced by Zen Buddhism, which is an important part of Japanese culture. Zen Buddhism is a form of Buddhism in which people strive to live "in the moment" and to appreciate the things in everyday life. Earlier tea ceremonies in Japan were held in great halls and were a chance for the wealthy to show off elaborate tea vessels.

Buddhist priests began incorporating the ideals of Zen into the tea ceremony. The ceremony was moved to small tea rooms and the equipment for preparing and serving tea became simpler. This was so that people became more aware of their surroundings and actions. By the 1500s, the tea ceremony had evolved into Sado, or Chado, as it is known and practiced today. Sado means "the way of tea." The tea ceremony represents four important Japanese beliefs: harmony, respect, purity, and tranquility.

The Ceremony

The Japanese tea ceremony lasts up to four hours. Each action and moment of the ceremony is carefully planned and carried out. The tea ceremony takes place in homes and at tea houses across Japan. A special room called a chashitsu, or tea room, is reserved for the ceremony. The host of the ceremony rings a bell or bangs on a gong, called a dora, to tell the guests that it is time to enter the room. In some tea ceremonies, guests are served a light meal before the ceremony begins. The ceremony includes the acts of serving and receiving tea, and all guests share tea from the same bowl. Throughout the ceremony, the host and the guests remember that their time together is a singular event that will never happen exactly the same way again.

▲ *An incense burner.*

The tea ceremony requires very specific tools, called dogu.

◀ *Matcha is Japanese powdered green tea used in the tea ceremony.*

◀ *A furo is a portable stove or fire pot to boil the water for tea.*

▼ *A fukusa is a silk cloth used for cleaning the tea container and scoop.*

▶ *A chasen is a bamboo whisk for mixing tea and water.*

▲ *Chashaku is a bamboo tea scoop used to dispense tea.*

Growing and Harvesting Tea

Today, most new tea plants are grown from cuttings of mature, or grown, plants. A cutting is usually a branch and a leaf. New plants are grown in greenhouses where temperature and **humidity** are controlled so that they will grow quickly. After about six months, or when the plants are six to eight inches (15 to 20 cm) tall, they are transplanted to fields. Another common way to grow new plants is by "branch layering." In this method, a branch from a mature plant is bent down into the soil. Over time, this branch takes root and becomes its own plant. It is then severed, or cut, from the original plant and replanted elsewhere on the plantation or farm.

New Growth

After about five years, the leaves of new tea plants are ready to be harvested for the first time. The plants will continue to produce leaves suitable for making tea for up to 50 years. While the plants are growing, they are sprayed with chemicals called pesticides to keep harmful insects that could kill the tea plants away. The tops of the plants are pruned back so they begin to spread outward, instead of growing taller. This creates what is called the "plucking table." Pruning makes the new leaves and buds tenderer than the leaves of trees that grow wild, and also makes it easier for the pickers to reach.

(below) Japanese tea farms look different than other tea farms. The plants are cultivated in long rows and are pruned so that the tops of the plants are curved.

Tea Harvest

Tea plants grow faster at some times of the year than at others. The number of times the plants produce new buds and leaves and the number of times leaves can be harvested varies depending on where the plants are grown. In some parts of the world, plants have a **dormant** winter period and a growing season. Tea plants grown in warmer parts of the world grow throughout the year, and leaves are picked as often as once a week during harvest.

Tea Pickers

Harvesting tea leaves is called "plucking." Many workers are required during the plucking season. Most tea harvesters are women. On some tea farms, mechanical shears are used to harvest the leaves, but they pick too many leaves at one time and can damage the crop. Picking tea by hand is the best way because only the bud and top two leaves are removed.

▾ *Tea pickers carry large baskets on their backs that are supported by bands across their foreheads. The leaves are put into the baskets as they are harvested.*

A Day in the Life

Each day, tea pickers have a quota, or set amount of tea leaves they must pick. Often, this quota is very high and pickers have to work nine hours a day to reach it. At the end of each day, the pickers carry their baskets many miles to have them weighed. Experienced pickers harvest as many as 66 pounds (30 kg) of leaves a day, for which they may only be paid $4. Tea pickers work in hot, steamy tea fields, among snakes and insects. Many do not have proper protective clothes to wear.

From Tea Factory to Tea Cup

Harvested tea leaves are brought to tea factories for processing. Processing is the steps taken to get a food or drink ready to use. The tea leaves are first withered, which reduces the amount of moisture in the leaves and makes their sap, or juices, stronger. Withering is done by spreading the leaves out thinly on trays and leaving them to dry in an airy, dry space in the factory for 24 hours. In areas where the climate is not suitable, the leaves are withered on racks or troughs by having hot air blown over them for about 16 hours. After withering, the leaves are put into a machine that crushes, rolls, and breaks them up.

Fermentation

Crushed tea leaves are left to ferment on large trays in a **humid** room. During fermentation, the sap in the leaves mixes with the air. This is a chemical process called oxidation, or fermentation. During fermentation, the leaves turn dark brown. Black tea and oolong tea are fermented, but green tea is not. After several hours, when the fermented leaves are the right color and odor, they are placed in drying chambers, where hot air is blown over them to make them crisp. Drying prevents any more fermentation from taking place.

(left) Tea leaves are spread out on trays for withering. When tea leaves are plucked, they contain up to 80 percent water. Through the processing stages, this moisture is reduced.

▶ *Black tea, shown far right, is left to ferment the longest, which is why it is darker in color than other types of tea.*

Grading

The next step in tea processing is grading the leaves, or sorting them according to size. Mechanical sieves with different sized holes are used to do the grading. The largest pieces are called "broken leaf" and are the most valuable. "Fannings" are smaller pieces, and the remaining tiny bits, called "dust," are used in tea bags.

(above) A tea worker grades tea by hand in the Southeast Asian country of Myanmar.

◄ In factories, tea is graded by machines and stored in tubs for packaging.

Tea Auctions

From the tea factory, tea is shipped to warehouses until an auction is held to sell the tea. At an auction, tea is bought and sold by tea **brokers**. Tea brokers work for either the seller or for the tea company that is buying the tea. The tea buyer who offers the highest price, or bid, gets the tea. Once the tea has been sold, it is packed into large wooden chests lined with aluminum foil. The aluminum makes the chest airtight, which means it keeps in the flavor and freshness of the tea. Tea loses its freshness if exposed to air for too long. The chests of tea are shipped on large cargo ships around the world. Some tea auctions today are offshore, which means the auction takes place on ships. Tea can also be sold directly from the tea factory to a tea company.

(below) A tea auction in Kenya. In the past, tea was sold to merchants who took the tea back to Europe and auctioned it from there. In 1861, the first auction was held in a producer country.

At the Tea Company

After the tea has been sold and shipped, it arrives at the tea company factory. There, tea leaves are blended, or mixed with other teas. Tea blenders are also tea tasters. They mix teas and flavorings together to make specialty teas. Their job is to make one brand, or type, of tea consistent, or the same, from package to package. This is because the quality of a tea crop varies from year to year, and can taste different depending on which plantation or farm it came from. Tea blends contain as many as 35 different types of tea. The teas are mixed in a large revolving drum. Then it is sifted, packaged, and sold to stores.

(above) Women package tea at a tea company factory in Egypt.

(below) A tea tester at a London, England, tea factory.

Tea Tasters

Tea tasters are hired by tea companies, which are companies that package and sell the tea to consumers. At auctions, tea tasters sample the different types of teas being sold from different tea plantations and farms. It takes many years of experience and training in the tea industry to be a tea taster. Tasters have to know the processes of growing and making tea. Before the auction begins, samples of tea are brewed and lined up for tea tasters to try. Tea tasters do not swallow the tea, but swish it around in their mouths and then spit it out. They do this so that one sample will not affect the next. A tea taster may sample hundreds of teas at a single auction. They comment on the taste and smell of each tea.

Types of Tea

There are hundreds of different types of teas available today. Many have different herbs or aromatic oils mixed in. Here are some of the main types of tea:

◀ Green Tea

Green tea is the most popular tea in China and Japan.

Black Tea

Black tea is fermented tea. It contains more caffeine than other types of tea.

Oolong Tea

Oolong tea is also known as semi-fermented tea. To make oolong tea, the leaves are wilted in the sun, and then shaken in baskets to bruise the edges of the leaves. The bruising helps the leaves ferment. The leaves are spread to dry until they are yellow and the edges are red. After about two hours, fermentation is stopped and the leaves are dried. Most oolong tea comes from Taiwan and China.

White Tea

White tea is also known as "silver tip" because the leaves have a silvery appearance. To make white tea, only unopened new buds are used. Most white tea comes from China and Sri Lanka. White tea has less caffeine than other types of tea and has a light and sweet taste.

▶ Scented and Flavored Teas

Green, oolong, and black teas are used to make scented and flavored teas. To make scented tea, processed tea is stored with flower blossoms or the essential oils of fruits, just before it is packaged at factories. These change the taste and smell of the tea. Teas are scented with flowers such as jasmine, and fruits such as orange, mango, and lemon. Flavored teas differ from scented teas because the flavorings are added during processing. Black current and Christmas tea, or tea flavored with cinnamon, cloves, and orange peel, are examples of flavored teas.

▼ Compressed Tea

Compressed tea is made into cakes, or bricks. In the past, fresh tea leaves were steamed and then pressed into cakes and dried. Today, most compressed tea is made from tea dust that is squeezed by machines into two pound (one kilogram) bricks. Compressed tea is made into a drink in Tibet and Mongolia, and eaten with butter and cheese.

The Future of Tea

The ancient Chinese were long aware of the health benefits of drinking tea. Modern scientists have also studied tea for its medicinal, or health benefits. Researchers have found that drinking tea may reduce the risk of cancer. Cancer is a deadly disease that has no cure. Scientists also believe that the caffeine in tea is good for the body's heart and circulatory system, which may help prevent heart disease and stroke. Tea is believed to help clean toxins, or poisonous substances, from the body.

Fair Trade Tea

Today, some tea consumers are becoming more aware of the benefits of purchasing fair trade tea. Fair trade is a movement that promotes fair prices and practices between producers and consumers. Under fair trade, tea buyers purchase tea directly from small groups of farmers and the tea is then sold to consumers through catalogs or at special stores.

Organic Tea

Fair trade tea also supports organic tea growing. In organic farming, workers are not subjected to the chemical pesticides and fertilizers that damage health as they are sprayed on the crops. Instead, animal manure, compost, organic matter, and ground cover are used to add nutrients to the soil. Insects such as lady bugs and spiders are used to prevent infestations of harmful pests instead of using pesticides. Many tea producing countries, such as India, China, Sri Lanka, and Vietnam, have organic tea farms today.

▲ *Boxes of fair trade tea are marked with this symbol. The money from fair trade tea goes to tea producers for pension funds, improved education and work training, fairer wages, and medical programs for workers.*

(above) Some of the many varieties of tea.

Tea Boards

In some countries, tea boards promote and regulate their country's tea industry. Some tea boards also guarantee the quality of tea. For example, the Tea Board of India developed logos that are attached to packages of tea to ensure that the tea was grown where the producer claims it was. For example, Darjeeling tea is a highly valued tea for its taste, and it is only grown in the Darjeeling area of India. To certify that a type of tea is from this region, the Tea Board of India developed a logo of the profile of a woman that is printed on packages containing pure Darjeeling tea. In Sri Lanka, the Tea Board developed a logo of a lion. Tea marked with this label on its packaging is guaranteed to have qualities set out by the Sri Lanka Tea Board.

▲ *Organic tea is grown without using chemical fertilizers and pesticides.*

(above) A tea worker waters young tea plants on a plantation.

Glossary

brokers Agents who make deals between buyers and sellers

Buddhist A person who follows the teachings of the Buddha and the religion of Buddhism, which teaches right conduct, wisdom, and meditation

buds Undeveloped plant parts, such as new shoots, flowers, or leaves

cells Basic units of life that make up all living things and their parts

climate The weather conditions of a certain region over the year

colonists Settlers from a ruling country who move to a new land

consumers The buyers and users of goods

convulsions Seizures, or involuntary muscle jerking in the body

dormant In a period of rest

elevation Height above sea level

epilepsy A brain disorder that results in seizures

evergreen shrub A bush that keeps its leaves all year round

exports Trade sent abroad

fermented Having been through the chemical process that takes place in certain plants

humidity The amount of moisture in the air

investors People who support a business venture in hopes of making more money

markets The commercial, or buying and selling, activities of a product

meditation The act of quietly sitting, relaxing, and clearing the mind of all normal thoughts

monasteries Where monks live and work

monks Members of a religious community who often live apart from the rest of society

monopoly Control over a product or service

porcelain Ceramic material for dishes

processed The steps a material is put through to get it ready for human consumption

prospered Became wealthy

social classes The economic rank of people within a society

standard Usual or common

staple A basic food or commodity

temples Places of worship

working class A group in society that works for wages, usually in factories

World's Fair A large exposition, or exhibition

Index

Printed in the U.S.A.